W9-BAF-583

Dragon in the Rocks

A story based on the childhood
of early paleontologist Mary Anning

written and illustrated by

MARIE DAY

Owl Books

Owl Books are published by Greey de Pencier Books Inc., 179 John Street, Suite 500, Toronto, Ontario M5T 3G5

OWL and the Owl colophon are trademarks of Owl Communications.
Greey de Pencier Books Inc. is a licensed user of trademarks of Owl Communications.

Text and illustrations © 1992 Marie Day
First paperback edition, 1995
All rights reserved. No part of this book may be reproduced or copied in any form without written consent from the publisher.

Distributed in the United States by Firefly Books (U.S.) Inc., 230 Fifth Avenue, Suite 1607, New York, NY 10001.

This book was published with the generous support of the Canada Council, the Ontario Arts Council and the Government of Ontario through the Ontario Publishing Centre.

Dedication
For Naomi and Vanessa

Canadian Cataloguing in Publication Data
Day, Marie
   Dragon in the rocks : a story based on the
childhood of early paleontologist Mary Anning

ISBN 0-920775-76-4 (bound)   ISBN 1-895688-38-8 (pbk.)

1. Anning, Mary, 1799–1847 - Juvenile fiction.
2. Paleontology - England - Juvenile fiction.
I. Title.

PS8557.A94D7 1992   jC813'.54   C91-095591-3
PZ7.D38Dr 1992

Design & Art Direction: Julia Naimska

Printed in Hong Kong

A   B   C   D   E   F

MILLIONS OF YEARS AGO WHEN DINOSAURS ROAMED THE EARTH, strange creatures swam in the sea. When they died, sand covered them where they lay on the ocean floor. Time passed. The ocean boiled and bubbled. Volcanoes erupted underwater, and the floor of the sea heaved up to form great cliffs.

Those ancient creatures vanished forever, and the cliffs became covered with trees and grass and wildflowers. Then people appeared. They settled in the pleasant places overlooking the sea. Two hundred years ago, in a little English seaside town called Lyme Regis, Mary Anning was born.

Mary grew up in a small house with her mother and father, her brother Joseph and her dog Tray. Early each morning Mary helped her mother make bread while Joseph helped his father saw wood in his workshop.

The little house smelled of fresh bread and new-cut wood and fragrant flowers, for Mary's mother always kept a bouquet on the table.

Mary's father made furniture to earn a living, but what he really liked best was collecting fossils. In those days a lot of people spent their time puzzling over these strange objects they found lying on the beach and buried in the cliff. There were odd-looking fish skeletons, giant seashells and even plants, all as hard as stone. How did they get there? Could these fossils be clues to the unknown world of long, long ago?

Mary and her father often went down the steep path to the beach. She loved the smell of the salt air and the sound of pounding waves. Sometimes, after a heavy rain, huge chunks of clay would fall from the cliff and crack apart as they landed on the shore. When Mary and her father examined the pieces they found mysterious bones and shells stuck inside them.

Mary learned from her father how to chip the rock-hard clay with a chisel and split it with a special little hammer. If she did it just right, a fossil would slide from the rock almost as easily as a baked cake slides from a greased pan. Mary's mother proudly placed the finest fossils on the mantelpiece where everyone could admire them.

"And where is my girl when I need help with sweeping floors or collecting eggs from under the hens?" she often said with a smile. "She's down at the shore collecting fossils!"

It was true. Every day, as soon as school was over, Mary wanted to rush down to the beach to search for treasure from the cliffs.

Mr. and Mrs. Anning sold many things on a stand in front of their house: lace and bonnets made by Mary's mother, tables and chairs made by Mary's father and Joseph, strange objects that Mary and her father had collected. "Come buy a fossil," Mary's father would cry. "The bone of an ancient crocodile! A flower, now turned to stone, that waved its petals at the bottom of the sea when the world was young!"

"Come buy a treasure, " Mary would echo. "The tooth of a cruel shark that lived long ago! A shell that sparkles like gold!"

All their lives, Mary and Joseph had heard about a huge fossil trapped in the cliff. The great, grinning creature lay in a faraway cove where the sea crashed and foamed. Their father had been there.

Many an evening he would tell them about the strange creature in the rocks.

"Its teeth are like razors and its eyes as big as saucers," their father would begin. "It's waiting there now, grinning in the dark. It looks like a dragon. Its body is as long as a rowboat, and its head as long as a man."

"Take me there, Father," Mary always begged. "Please!"

Joseph wasn't nearly as eager. "Why get so excited over some old fish bones?" he would scoff.

It would be hard to count the number of nights Mary asked her father to tell about his journey to find the dragon. Again and again she heard about the treacherous climb up the slippery black cliff, how the sea soaked him through, how frightened he was, how he shivered with cold. How, when he was ready to give up, he saw the thing right above his head and stared into its great eye at last.

Mary longed for the day when she would see the giant dragon for herself.

One cold rainy morning Mary went down to the shore with Tray. Her father was very ill and could not leave his bed to search for fossils.

"Halloo, Mary," a voice rang out. It was her father's good friend, Captain Fossy. Everyone called him Captain Fossy because he spent every morning, noon and evening collecting fossils on the beach. His wide plumed hat had fossil shells sewn all over it. Captain Fossy had seen the great dragon too, and he said when she was big enough he'd go with Mary and her father to find it again.

As always, Captain Fossy rummaged in the deep pockets of his coat and brought out a present. "Something very special today, Mary," he said. He put a lovely, flat round stone in her hand. "A dragon's eye, I'm sure it is. Take it along and show your father."

"Oh, thank you, Captain Fossy. Father is so sick, and it will cheer him up," said Mary.

Mary came home to find the house strangely quiet. She held the dragon's eye stone tight in her hand. Tray wagged his tail anxiously and looked up at her. They both knew something had happened.

Then Mary heard the sound of someone coming downstairs. It was the doctor carrying his black bag, followed by her mother and Joseph, whose face was red from crying. The doctor put his hand on Mary's shoulder and patted it gently. "You must be brave, Mary," he said, "for your father has left us forever."

After a week had passed, Mary's mother spoke through her tears. "We are poor people. What will become of us?"

"I will go to the town of Axminster, where there is plenty of work," said Joseph. "It is not too far, and I will send money home every week." And Mary said, "Don't worry, Mother. I will leave school and spend all day finding fossils. Tray will help. We will sell them just as we always have. I know that is what Father would want."

Soon Mary was very busy. While her mother sold lace and bonnets on the stand outside the house, Mary went each day to find strange and wonderful fossils down at the shore. She took her discoveries to the busy place where the passenger coaches stopped to give the horses a rest on the way to Axminster.

While the horses rested, the passengers got out to stretch their legs, and Mary displayed her basket of fossils for sale. The ladies and gentlemen often left her with an empty basket and her pockets full of coins. Joseph sent money, as he had promised, and he came home often.

One fine summer morning when Joseph was visiting, he and Mary decided to go down to the beach. They stopped for a few moments on the cliff and watched the puffy clouds passing by in the blue sky. Suddenly they heard someone calling their names from the shore below.

It was Captain Fossy. "The weather is perfect for dragon-hunting," he shouted up to them. "The sea is calm as glass and the wind is steady."

Mary grabbed Joseph's hand, and they flew down the path to the shore. Tray jumped and barked alongside them. They were going to see the great fossil at last. Teeth like razors and eyes as big as saucers!

Captain Fossy led Mary and Joseph a long, long way along the rocky beach, and then they began to climb the steep, wet cliff. They clambered high over dark, slimy rocks and down past caves full of black shadows and crashing waves. Mary's heart beat fast as they edged across a narrow, slippery clay ledge that threatened to break off suddenly and fall into the sea. When they stopped to catch their breath, Mary looked back towards Lyme Regis. It was so far away the houses looked like little toys.

"When will we be there, Captain Fossy?" she asked. Captain Fossy shook his head. "I don't know," he said, gazing out to sea. "And now the wind is coming up. See, the tide is rising too! We'll have to turn back."

Just then Tray started to bark from somewhere right above them.

"There it is, there, look up!" Joseph shouted.

Half buried in the dark rock was the largest skeleton Mary had ever seen.
It was more strange than the dragon in her dreams. It was as long as a
rowboat. Its huge mouth was bigger than her whole body, and full of razor-
sharp teeth. Its eye was much bigger than a saucer. It was bigger than her
mother's biggest plate, the one that the Christmas goose was served on.

"We must go," Captain Fossy said. "Hurry now. The tide is rising fast." Mary was so entranced that she hardly heard him. When Joseph took her hand and pulled her away, she realized with a start that ocean waves were dashing over her feet.

The journey back was hard. More than once they had to scramble up the cliff as the waves grew stronger and crashed into foam just beneath them. When they arrived home, it was very late. Mary's mother scolded as she wrapped them in her warm shawl.

As Mary and Joseph dried themselves by the fire, they described every moment of their adventure. "I'm going to dig it out of the cliff. I know I can, " said Mary when they'd finished their tale.

"Oh no, you can't, " said Joseph. "It's huge, Mother, far too big a fossil for her to tackle."

"Nonsense, Joseph," their mother replied. "If your sister is determined to dig that creature out of the cliff, she will."

Soon, every fine day, Mary could be seen making her way down the beach. She always wore her father's old hat, to bring her luck. Little Tray was by her side. He liked to carry her basket of tools up and down the cliff.

While the tide was low, Mary chipped away at the rocks. When she'd carved out a few chunks, she would take them to a sheltered stretch of beach. There she hammered and pried at the rock-hard clay until the bones within were freed. Back to the skeleton she'd climb again, to start all over.

The weeks and months went by. The work was hard. As the hidden parts of the huge sea creature slowly emerged from the clay, Mary asked herself questions about it.

What was her dragon like when it was alive? What color was it? Green? Blue? Red? Striped, like a sunfish? What did it eat, down deep in the ocean? Even as it hunted, did even bigger creatures hunt for *it*? Was one of *them* trapped in the rocks, waiting now for her hammer to release it?

Mary had a plan to put the great creature together again. She had drawn a picture of the whole skeleton as best she could, and had given a number to each bone. Now as she chipped each bone from the rock, she numbered it. Then she carefully wrapped each one in plaster and cloth to protect it.

The baskets she carried back to her father's workshop at sunset each day were very heavy.

Sometimes strong stonecutters came to help Mary. They were used to hard work. They laughed and sang as they helped her chip the bones out of the rocks. They teased Mary with a tongue-twisting chant: *She sells seashells by the seashore.* It made her smile, even when she was very tired and her body ached from head to toe.

Finally, she pried the very last bone from the steep clay cliff.

Mary set to work cleaning the last bits of rock from each bone with small files and brushes. When that was done, she began to put the creature's bones together again like a huge jigsaw puzzle. She had numbered each bone so carefully that the creature took shape almost like magic on the floor of her father's workshop. Her mother brought her meals to her there, for she would not leave until the giant fossil was complete.

Word travelled all the way to the great city of London about a little girl who had dug a huge ancient creature out of a cliff. Many people didn't believe the story. How in the world could a child of twelve do that?

One day, five important scientists came all the way from London to see Mary. They crowded into her father's workshop and marvelled over the giant fossil. They were amazed to see how perfectly Mary had arranged the creature's bones, just as they had been in the clay. They could hardly believe their own eyes.

"Please tell me, what is this creature I have found?" Mary asked eagerly. The scientists explained that she had unearthed the rare skeleton of an ichthyosaur, a giant fish-lizard that had lived in the ocean millions of years ago. Like a whale, this mighty animal came to the surface for air. It had looked something like a dolphin, only much, much bigger, of course.

"Will you allow me to buy this remarkable fossil?" asked one of the men. "I'd like to take it to a famous museum in London where thousands of people can see it." Mary nearly cried from joy. How proud Father would have been of her!

That night, all the neighbors gathered on the beach to celebrate with Mary. Joseph brought a present for his sister, a chair that he had made himself, covered in red satin. Mary's mother gave her a lovely lace collar to wear. There was plenty of cake and cider and lots of singing. The blacksmith played his fiddle and the schoolmaster joined in with his accordion. Tray ran around and around in excitement.

Captain Fossy raised his cup high and shouted, "A toast to Mary, the greatest of all the fossil seekers!" Everyone clapped and cheered.

As the moon set and the stars became brighter, the people of Lyme Regis were still singing and dancing and talking about the great ichthyosaur. Mary was very happy. She just knew that there were other wonderful creatures to be discovered in the cliff. The next day she was going to set out to find them.

Mary Anning was a real person. With the help of her mother she continued to search for fossils, and she spent the rest of her life digging in the cliffs at Lyme Regis for mysterious creatures from the past. When you hear the tongue-twister "She sells seashells by the seashore," think of Mary Anning, for it is said that the "she" who sold the shells was her. And if you go to the Natural History Museum in London, look for a creature with teeth like razors and an eye much bigger than your mother's biggest plate—the one that the holiday meal is served on; and if the creature is longer than four men put together and has flippers shaped like paddles, then you too have found Mary's dragon in the rocks.